DOLLARS AND SENSE

A GUIDE TO FINANCIAL LITERACY ™

Taxes and Government Spending

CLIVE NICHOLS AND
MARIE BUSSING-BARKS

rosen publishing's
rosen
central®

NEW YORK

Published in 2012 by The Rosen Publishing Group, Inc.
29 East 21st Street, New York, NY 10010

Copyright © 2012 by The Rosen Publishing Group, Inc.

First Edition

Library of Congress Cataloging-in-Publication Data

Nichols, Clive.
Taxes and government spending/Clive Nichols, Marie Bussing-Barks.
    p. cm.—(Dollars and sense)
Includes bibliographical references and index.
ISBN 978-1-4488-4714-3 (library binding)—
ISBN 978-1-4488-4725-9 (pbk.)—
ISBN 978-1-4488-4757-0 (6-pack)
1. Taxation—United States—Juvenile literature. 2. Government spending policy—
United States—Juvenile literature. 3. Fiscal policy—United States—Juvenile literature.
I. Bussing-Burks, Marie, 1958– II. Title. III. Series.
HJ2381.N53 2012
336.73—dc22

                                                                2011006197

Manufactured in the United States of America

CPSIA Compliance Information: Batch #S11YA: For further information, contact Rosen Publishing, New York, New York, at 1-800-237-9932.

CONTENTS

We know that the government spends a lot. But where does it get all that money? Most government spending is financed by taxes. So in many ways, the government earns and spends money much like an individual or a business. The difference is that the ways in which the government collects and disperses funds is much more complex. There are many different types of taxation, and the way the government spends money is closely watched by citizens and politicians alike. The reason is that the ways we tax and spend as a nation are critical to the health of the economy and the well-being of the country as a whole.

We need the government because it provides us with important goods and services, the kinds of goods and services that individuals and private companies do not have the resources to provide. You use government goods and services every day. The highways, public education systems, and the national defense are all government functions. Even your local subway or city bus system is a government service. Your grandparents are happy to get their monthly Social Security retirement check, and they have the government to thank for that, too. For these reasons, the government is a big spender. About one-third of all the money disbursed in the United States every year is spent by the government.

There are actually three levels of government: federal, state, and local. The spending habits of each are quite different, although all levels provide goods and services that are impractical for individuals or businesses to supply. According to estimates, the U.S. federal government spent around $3.7 trillion in 2010. Health care is the biggest expense. National defense is next in line. Third is pensions.

Other large expenses on the federal level include net interest (the fee the government must pay when it borrows money), Medicare (a medical plan to help seniors), and health programs. Foreign aid and veterans' benefits are among the many smaller spending items grouped in a separate category.

Now you know an important fact about economic activity in the United States. Not all spending is carried on by individuals and businesses. Much commerce is conducted by federal, state, and local governments. Therefore, the government is an important provider of many essential goods and services that we use every day.

CHAPTER **ONE**

UNDERSTANDING TAXES

According to the White House, the federal government collected over $2.1 trillion in taxes in 2009. The largest source of revenue for the federal government comes from personal, individual income taxes. Every April 15, your father, mother, uncle, aunt, and grandparents pay a part of the income they earned during the prior year to the Internal Revenue Service (IRS). It is a legal obligation, if you earn over a certain base level of income.

Social Security payroll taxes are the second biggest source of federal income. Every person who works must give a portion of his or her paycheck to the Social Security fund. When workers retire, the money is paid back to them in the form of monthly retirement checks. Corporate income tax is the next big source of revenue. Businesses must pay a share of their profits to the federal government. Other revenue items include excise taxes on gasoline, alcohol, and cigarettes, and custom duties on imported goods.

State and local governments collect a great deal of money from taxes. Sales tax is the largest category. Most state governments collect a sales tax on goods and services sold in the state.

Secondly, the federal government transfers some of its income to state and local governments to spend. Local governments also benefit from the third-greatest revenue source:

Taxes on products such as tobacco help the government fund public resources like roads, military defense, and Social Security.

property taxes. Property taxes are payments based on the value of your home or land. Fourth and fifth, respectively, are the income taxes individuals and businesses pay to state and local governments. Utility taxes and income from invested funds from employee pensions are some of the revenue sources in the "other" category.

There are different types of taxes. No matter what level of government collects the tax, all taxes can be described in one of three ways—progressive, proportional, or regressive.

The Progressive Tax

The federal tax on individuals and businesses is an example of a progressive tax. The more money a person or company makes, the greater the percentage paid in taxes. For example, current personal income tax rates start at 15 percent for moderate-income individuals and rise to nearly 40 percent for high-income earners.

The tax rates are progressive because high-income earners pay a larger percentage in taxes. Those who think that a progressive tax is a good idea believe that people and businesses with more money should pay a proportionally greater amount. Others argue that this is unfair to those people and businesses who work hard and earn a lot.

The Proportional Tax

A proportional tax rate is one that remains the same, regardless of the size of one's income. A 4 percent proportional

If line 40 (taxable income) is—		And you are—			
At least	But less than	Single	Married filing jointly *	Married filing separately	Head of a household
		Your tax is—			
44,000					
44,000	44,050	7,816	5,904	7,816	6,701
44,050	44,100	7,829	5,911	7,829	6,714
44,100	44,150	7,841	5,919	7,841	6,726
44,150	44,200	7,854	5,926	7,854	6,739
44,200	44,250	7,866	5,934	7,866	6,751
44,250	44,300	7,879	5,941	7,879	6,764
44,300	44,350	7,891	5,949	7,891	6,77
44,350	44,400	7,904	5,956	7,904	6,78
44,400	44,450	7,916	5,964	7,916	6,80
44,450	44,500	7,929	5,971	7,929	6,8
44,500	44,550	7,941	5,979	7,941	6,
44,550	44,600	7,954	5,986	7,954	6,
44,600		7,966	5,994	7,966	6
44,650				7,979	
44,700					
44,750					
44,800					
	44,900		6,041		6,039

The amount a person pays in taxes depends on the type of tax structure that's in place. Currently, Americans pay a percentage of federal taxes based on how much they earn.

tax on an income of $10,000 would be $400. If you made $100,000, you would still pay only 4 percent, so your bill would be $4,000. Only a few states tax individuals at a proportional rate. Pennsylvania used a proportional income tax rate of 3.07 percent in 2011 according to the Pennsylvania Department of Revenue. Most states have progressive income tax rates.

Some individuals like this kind of tax because it treats everyone equally. Everyone has the same tax rate. Many who favor proportional taxes think that it would be fairer and easier than our complex federal progressive tax.

The Regressive Tax

Most taxes, other than income taxes, are regressive. With a regressive tax, the higher the income, the smaller the percentage of income paid as taxes. Most states charge sales taxes, which are regressive in relation to income. Sales taxes are calculated as a percentage of the selling price of goods and services. State sales taxes vary a great deal. Examples include a 3 percent sales tax in Colorado and a 6 percent sales tax in Florida.

Let's look at an example in which the state sales tax is 5 percent. The Johnson family makes $50,000 a year and spends $20,000 for living expenses, while the Wilson family makes $20,000 and spends their entire income on necessities. Both the Johnsons and the Wilsons pay $1,000 in sales tax (5 percent of $20,000). A closer look shows that the

Tax laws can vary from state to state. Certain states may offer lower taxes to entice people to spend more money and boost the economy.

Johnsons pay only 1/50th of their total income in sales tax, while the Wilsons pay 1/20th of their total income in sales tax.

Lower income earning families like the Wilsons generally spend a greater fraction of their earnings on sales tax. Lower income families are therefore burdened by progressive taxes. Those who argue against a regressive tax say that it is unfair to the poor because it requires them to spend a larger portion of their income on basic needs.

BILLS, NOTES, AND BONDS

Bills, notes, and bonds are other ways the government receives funding. Treasury bills are short-term securities that mature, that is, come due for payment, in one year or less. These securities are high-priced. The minimum amount is $10,000. The Treasury bill interest rate is a widely watched rate. Many business and consumer loans are based on the Treasury bill rate. Often these loans are a few points higher than the Treasury rate and vary with that rate.

Treasury notes are intermediate federal securities with maturities that range from one to ten years. Notes range from $1,000 to $5,000. Interest rates for notes are slightly higher than for bills. Investors wait longer to get their money back, so they demand a higher interest rate.

While the Federal Reserve can print money, doing so can lead to inflation. Another way it raises money is by issuing bills, notes, and bonds.

Treasury bonds are issued in units of $1,000. Maturities range from ten to thirty years. Interest rates for Treasury bonds are generally higher than rates for bills or notes. Investors loan the federal government money for a long time when they buy bonds. In turn, investors expect a higher interest rate.

U.S. savings bonds are issued in amounts ranging from $50 to $10,000. Because they are more reasonably priced, many consumers enjoy investing in savings bonds. They also make great gifts for birthdays, anniversaries, and graduations.

If you own a bond, you own a piece of the national debt. Treasury bills, notes, and bonds are marketable securities. You can trade the securities with other investors before they mature. That way, if needed, you can get your money back before the issuance matures. Savings bonds are nonmarketable. You can't trade them with other investors, but you can cash them in at your local banking institution.

The major problem in organizing a fair tax system is determining who will pay the tax. Our government has decided that a just system requires a combination of these three forms of taxes.

Which System Is Best?

There has been debate throughout history over which tax system is best, and the debate will likely continue well into the future. The reason is that no tax system is perfect. Taxation is a complicated

State income tax structures often vary from state to state. Many fiscal decisions are made by the state's budget committee, such as this one in Austin, Texas.

OGDEN

ZAFFIRINI

arrangement between a government and its citizens. There is one government that serves many different types of people from all economic classes. If a rich person and a poor person use the same tax-funded road, how much tax should each person pay for it? Should the amount be calculated by the person's income, as in a tax bracket, or should it be a flat rate, as in a toll? If it is a flat rate, then is everyone really paying the same amount since every dollar a poor person pays is a greater percentage of income than a rich person would pay? These are debates that cross not only financial but ethical lines, which make the tax debate so long-lasting.

Aside from the different tax systems of progressive, proportional, and regressive, most of the debate over taxes is simply about lower taxes versus higher taxes and which is better for the economy.

The Argument for Lower Taxes

The argument for lower relative taxes is based on the economic philosophy that the less people pay in taxes, the more money they have in their pockets to spend on goods and services, which therefore stimulates the economy. This is a view generally argued for by those who are politically conservative.

The idea of lower taxes is usually associated with an economic theory called "trickle-down economics," or "supply-side economics." Both these philosophies argue that by allowing those in a society who are wealthy enough to produce goods and services, "supply," they will help the economy as a whole by having the benefits of producing goods and services trickle down to the lower classes. Lower taxes make it easier to create supply. It gives the public the money to invest in businesses that create goods and services.

Part of the argument of those who are against lower taxes is that it unfairly rewards the rich and punishes the poor. The reason is that the rich pay the most taxes, both proportionally and as a fixed amount. Therefore, lowering taxes would save the most money for rich people, money that could be used for social programs that benefit the poor. Additionally, some people feel that as an ethical issue, the people who have the most money should be more responsible for sharing that wealth.

The Argument for Higher Taxes

The opposing viewpoint of higher taxes is rooted in the belief that the better way to stimulate the economy is by increasing the revenue of the federal government—in other words, increasing the amount it receives from taxes. The government can then use this money to pay down the national debt and invest in government-supported businesses such as energy, education, and infrastructure. These government-supported programs benefit all in society. This view is generally supported by those who are politically liberal.

Those who are against higher taxes argue that it discourages investment because it decreases potential profit from investment. For example, an individual may not think that investing in a stock is worth the risk if the amount of the potential profits he or she would have to pay in taxes is too high. The same goes for businesses. People may choose not to start a business if they feel that too-high a portion of their profits would need to be paid in taxes, which instead could be used to hire employees or buy equipment that could grow the business.

CHAPTER TWO

WHAT IS GOVERNMENT SPENDING?

In terms of how it's supposed to budget, the government operates like a family. If a family spends more than it earns, it must borrow to make up the difference. So, too, must the government borrow. It could simply print all the money it needed, but that would lead to serious economic problems, such as uncontrollable inflation. Measuring how well the government is managing its budget, and if it needs to borrow, is fairly simple. Add up all the money collected during the year through taxes and other means and subtract all the money the government has spent during the year.

The first Continental Congress was held at Carpenter's Hall at a time when the fledgling nation was introduced to the notion of debt incurred from the Revolutionary War.

Understanding Debt

Just like any family, the government can go into debt. The huge national debt is not a new story. The United States first went into debt in 1790, when it assumed the Revolutionary War obligations of the Continental Congress. The debt was just over $75 million at the end of 1790. The first major increase in government debt occurred

BASIC ACCOUNTING

A new candidate for president promises, if elected, to spend more on new construction, national defense, and environmental programs. He also promises to reduce taxes. The business community is concerned about this proposal and has asked you to speak to the candidate on its behalf. But keeping this promise could hurt the country.

This presidential candidate needs to understand basic accounting, in the same way that families and individuals do. If the candidate increases the level of spending on construction, national defense, and the environment, he must finance this increased spending. He would actually need to raise, rather than reduce, taxes to cover the new expenses. If the candidate tried to keep his promise and raise spending and reduce taxes, the country would have to borrow even more money.

It is important that politicians remember the principles of basic accounting when making decisions about taxation and spending. Just like any individual, household, or business needs to make sure it doesn't spend more than it makes, the government needs to do the same to avoid financial problems down the road.

during World War II, when it rose from $40 billion to $279 billion. Our chance to reduce the debt was hindered by the Korean War in the early 1950s. The Vietnam War, which began in the mid-1960s, enlarged the debt even further. Early on, people were not concerned about the debt if it arose because of spending on war efforts.

In recent years, the United States has not faced a major war crisis. Still, the country's debt has grown rapidly. By 1980 the debt stood at $1 trillion. Today, in 2011, the debt of $14 trillion is drawing a lot of attention. Politicians and the public are beginning to ask whether the size of the national debt is beginning to threaten America's leadership role on the world stage with economies such as those of China and India rising so rapidly.

Impact on Future Generations

Some people argue that a rising debt burdens future generations, who must somehow pay back the money. Because there's little risk that the U.S. government is going to cease doing business, it is not necessary to repay the entire debt at any one time. Governments, in theory, never fail to pay what they owe. Future generations could continue borrowing. Future generations must, at least, tax themselves to pay the interest charges. The people who own the debt will receive those interest payment as income.

Another concern is that as the debt increases, interest payments alone may become a substantial portion of the federal government's spending package. This would force the

There are certain essential services that the government needs to fund, such as a police force to keep law and order.

government to reduce spending on other important goods and services.

The government may even have to borrow money to repay the debt. Businesses also borrow funds to build new factories, buy machinery, and hire more workers. Government borrowing takes away funds that would have been used by businesses. An increase in the debt results in more government goods at the expense of business-produced goods. This is a big concern for those who prefer a small government. Many economists agree that it is one of the key disadvantages of a rising debt.

Advantages

Let's not, however, forget about the benefits that occur because of the high debt. The government has provided us with many essential goods and services, and through massive spending it has lifted our economy out of depression and recession many times. The bonds and securities that the government uses to finance the debt provide many investors with secure savings instruments.

We know that the U.S. government owes $14 trillion. But where did the government borrow that much? Who would lend the federal government trillions of dollars? What are the secure savings instruments the government uses to borrow?

The U.S. government has financed the debt by selling bonds and securities. Part of the debt is held by government agencies, like the Social Security Administration, which invests its surplus in bonds and securities. The federal government borrows the rest from individuals, businesses, banking institutions, and foreigners. Fortunately, savers view government bonds and securities as excellent investments because they are a safe way to store money. The federal government always pays investors back. Government bonds and securities offer a good interest rate for the use of loaned money. There are four main types of bonds and securities sold by the U.S. Treasury: Treasury bills, Treasury notes, Treasury bonds, and savings bonds.

The Bank Bailouts

While adding to the national debt is considered negative by all political parties and nearly all people, there are times when spending is deemed necessary to avoid economic collapse. One of those times was in 2008.

America and the world came to an economic crossroads in that year. Several years of fiscal irresponsibility, ranging from

THE WORLD MARKET FOR U.S. DEBT

Luckily, because U.S. bonds and securities have so many great features, they are easy for the government to sell. Even businesses and companies outside the United States like our government securities and bonds. Foreign individuals and businesses held approximately 25 percent of the U.S. debt in 2007 according to MSNBC.

The other part is held internally. When debt is internal, the United States essentially owes the money to itself—an American business, banking institution, or government agency. The large percentage of debt that is owed to foreigners concerns some economists. This is a lot of money that must be paid back by Americans to people and businesses outside of the U.S. economy. That money ends up in other countries, adding to their economic growth, not ours.

overborrowing and overlending to risky financial bets by banks, led to one of the worst banking crises in memory. This was known as the "subprime crisis" for the risky loans that banks were offering homeowners. On March 14, 2008, the stock price of investment bank Bear Stearns plummeted due to a lack of confidence that the bank was in good financial health after its involvement with subprime mortgages, among other factors. Two days later, the storied financial institution was bought by the bank J. P. Morgan Chase for just a fraction of its value just days before.

This set in motion a domino effect of bank failures, bailouts, and mergers. The decision of the U.S. Federal Reserve to bail out certain banks, or save them from collapse by purchasing their assets, was a decision that saved some of the most powerful financial institutions in the world. The Troubled Asset Relief Fund (TARP) was signed into law by President George W. Bush on October 3, 2008, and allowed the U.S. government to use up to $700 billion to buy the assets of troubled banks. Without these institutions, the economy could have ground to a halt. Therefore, while the bailouts added hundreds of billions of dollars to the national debt, it may have saved the economy from ruin.

CHAPTER **THREE**

BUDGETING

For many people, the idea of budgeting their money is about as appealing as dieting. But diets often tell you exactly what to eat, whereas budgets do not tell you exactly how to spend your money.

A budget is a plan that is used by anyone, including individuals, businesses, and governments. A budget is used to help you live as well as possible with the money that you have. In the business world, budgets help managers plan as well as possible for their companies and employees.

One of the largest budgets you hear about is that of the United States. It is called the federal budget, and it is designed to keep track of how the government spends its money and collects its income (taxes and other revenues).

If taxes equal government spending, the budget is balanced. It is unusual for a government to have an exactly balanced budget. It is more common for a budget to have a deficit or surplus. If the government spends less than it collects, the budget has a surplus; if it spends more than it collects, the budget has a deficit.

Treasury Secretary Timothy Geithner's job involves directing the federal government's spending policy. He played a large role in responding to the financial crisis from 2007 to 2010.

Currently, the federal budget is unbalanced. This occurs in a budget when too much money is spent or not enough money is received. The result of an unbalanced budget is that there is not enough money to pay all of the bills. In order to balance the federal budget, members of the Congress pass measures regulating how funds are spent. It is obvious that a government needs to have a budget and keep track of how its money is spent and received.

THE FEDERAL BUDGET

Let's take a closer look at two important years: 1997, when the federal government still ran a deficit, and 1998, when a surplus budget appeared. Sure enough, in 1997, the federal government had a deficit. The government spent $21.9 billion more than it collected in taxes. But in 1998, the government showed a surplus by collecting $69.2 billion more than it spent. In 1999, the government had a $122.7 billion surplus. Surplus budgets continued to follow. Sounds good. Then what is all the fuss about? Why are so many people complaining about the federal government's budget? The answer is debt.

Just because the government runs a budget surplus in one year, it cannot forget about all those years that it had to borrow money. Hey, when you borrow, you have to pay it back. The government does, too. The debt is calculated by adding up all the previous annual deficits and subtracting any surpluses. And are you ready for the total? Drum roll, please. The national debt reached a total of $14 trillion in 2009. It will take a lot of surpluses to pay down such a large debt.

There are official names for the U.S. debt: the gross federal debt, the gross national debt, or the gross debt. Gross here doesn't mean ugly or uncool debt; it simply means the total debt.

People are concerned about a budget deficit because the government must borrow money to pay for its excess spending. The government is then in debt and must pay back what it owes with interest. You as a taxpayer are responsible for and will ultimately have to pay that debt. Budget surpluses, on the other hand, are generally viewed favorably. The government appears to be managing its money properly, and taxes may even be reduced.

State and local governments have historically done a pretty good job of balancing their budgets each year. However, with the economic downturn in 2008, many state and local governments struggled along with the nation as a whole.

Personal Budget Versus the Federal Budget

The federal budget is not that much different from your own personal budget. Simply put, a budget compares how much you spend and how much you save. While the government may create budgets for grand endeavors like national defense and health care, its budgets are calculated in much the same way as your budgets for things such as clothes and entertainment.

Perhaps you are saving money to buy a car. Your parents have told you that you must pay for part of the gas and the insurance. Now, you wonder if you will have enough money to pay for a car and these other costs. Maybe you want to go to college. However, you do not know if you are saving enough money. You like to have fun, too. Your friends are planning to see a movie and then have pizza on Saturday night. You are

Savings bonds are issued to individuals by the U.S. Treasury to raise money for the federal government. They're also good for helping individuals save money.

short on cash, but you do not want to ask your parents or a friend for money. Then, you remember some cash that you had tucked in your desk drawer for an emergency. Should you use that money to go out on Saturday?

Do you ever wonder where your money goes? Do you sometimes find that you cannot pay for the things you want? A budget takes the guesswork out of managing your money. Good budgets include income, expenses, and savings. Income is any money that you receive from someone or money that you earn. Earnings are money you receive for doing work. Income is money coming in. Expenses are money going out.

You might get income in a variety of ways. You might earn wages from a part-time job. You might get an allowance from a parent or guardian for doing regular chores around the house. Sometimes, you might be paid to do special projects, such as cleaning the attic or garage, or helping someone move. You might earn money by having a business that sells services, goods, or products. Services include babysitting, tutoring, mowing lawns, and walking dogs. Or, you might sell goods like handmade bird feeders or chopped firewood. What do you do with your income? Do you spend all of your money as soon as you get it? Or, do you save part or all of your income? Do you hide your savings under the bed or put it into a savings account at a bank?

Proper budgeting can help you reach your money goals. Income, savings, and expenses affect personal money goals. In addition, your money goals might not be the same as your friend's money goals. You might be saving to buy a car, while your friend is saving for a new computer and printer. Both are examples of long-term goals because buying a new car or computer generally costs more than a weekly paycheck or monthly allowance. Making and following a budget can help you reach your short-term and long-term money goals. A budget gives you a picture of where your money is going now and where it might go in the future. Budgeting can help you save your money. You can adjust your budget as your financial needs change.

CHAPTER FOUR

FISCAL POLICY

We know that the government provides us with goods and services. The government imposes taxes to raise money to pay for these goods and services. But wait. There is another reason that the government might want to tax and spend. It is called fiscal policy.

Fiscal policy is the government's plan for taxing and spending for the purpose of controlling the economy and its rate of expansion. It is designed to regulate the amount of spending by citizens and businesses by changing our available income. If the president and Congress feel that we should be spending more or less, they can organize a fiscal plan.

President Barack Obama stands with his economic team at the time, which included Lawrence Summers, director of the White House National Economic Council; Treasury Secretary Timothy Geithner; and Peter Orszag, director of the Office of Management and Budget.

What happens if people are spending too much money? Store owners won't be able to keep products on the shelves. They might even think they are not charging enough for their products and decide to raise prices. If workers begin to notice that store prices are rising, they will go to their bosses and ask for a raise. Hey, they need more money to buy those expensive items. And the spiral of wage and price increases continues. This is called inflation.

JOHN MAYNARD KEYNES

Economist John Maynard Keynes (1883–1946) was born in Cambridge, England. In his famous text published in 1936, *The General Theory of Employment, Interest, and Money*, Keynes attempted to explain the widespread unemployment during the Great Depression. He said that it was the government's responsibility to maintain high employment by spending on public works programs. His followers, the Keynesians, called this "fiscal policy." They encouraged taxes to increase economic activity.

President Roosevelt's New Deal administration spent several billion dollars on many programs and projects designed to put people to work. The programs did increase economic growth, as the New Deal gave millions of people jobs, and those people could then purchase more goods and services, stimulating businesses to produce more.

The ideas of British economist John Maynard Keynes profoundly affected macroeconomic practices during the Great Depression and continue to influence economic policy decisions today.

If the president and Congress feel that prices are rising too fast, they might use fiscal policy to dampen spending. Also called a contractionary policy, the plan would be to increase taxes or reduce government spending. Because the government is spending less, a tight policy reduces the amount of money in the economy available to purchase goods and services. Because taxes are increased, individuals and businesses have less money to spend on goods and services. This decreases the demand for goods and services and brings down prices.

The government might consider a different fiscal policy if the economy is not growing fast enough and there are not enough jobs. With an expansionary policy, the president and Congress call for increased government spending or reduced taxes. By spending more, the government pumps money into the economy and leaves individuals with more money to buy things like groceries, clothes, and new cars.

Businesses are left with more money to buy raw materials, build factories, and invest in new equipment. This creates a demand for additional production, and the economy expands. When the government reduces taxes, it is counting on individuals and businesses to spend more. If individuals and businesses decide to save the extra money, the economy will not be stimulated as the government intended.

Problems with Fiscal Policy

It would be great if fiscal policy were that easy—just change government spending or taxes, and the economy runs perfectly. In reality, there are several problems with fiscal policy.

The thing about spending to increase economic growth is that the government cannot get the money it needs through taxes. If it did, whatever money it put into the economy with one hand, it would be taking away with the other hand. Keynesian policy depends upon deficit spending, that is, you have to spend money you don't have. You have to borrow the money. When you have an expansionary fiscal policy and increase government spending, you must add to the government's debt.

Assume that the government feels that taxes or spending appropriations should be changed to produce a healthier economy. In a democracy like ours, with many competing interest groups, it can take months or years for a bill to pass through Congress. By the time a bill is passed, the economic situation may have changed. Some economists believe that the government can never get it right and only makes things worse.

What Can We Do?

We may all agree that the economy is not doing well, but the problem is knowing exactly how to fix it. Even economists can't always agree. To make it even more complicated, sometimes the economic data can be unclear. One government number might suggest that the economy is going strong, while another hints that we are headed for trouble.

There's no one reason why economies do well or poorly. However, experts know that consumer spending, or how much citizens spend at the cash register, is a strong driver of economic growth.

Some fiscal policy is automatic. Automatic fiscal policy does not require congressional legislation. For example, economic activity falls during a recession because people don't work as much. The government then pays more for unemployment insurance to those who don't have jobs. These people spend the money on groceries and other necessities of life, and economic activity is automatically energized.

Because fiscal policy is so complicated, the president and Congress rarely and reluctantly take an active role in adjusting government spending and taxes. Let's took at some historical examples and see how it worked out.

Early in 1963, President John F. Kennedy told the country that we were doing well but that we had not reached maximum income and employment levels. Kennedy used deficit spending to spur economic activity. At the same time, he requested a tax reduction on personal and corporate incomes. After Kennedy's death, President Lyndon B. Johnson signed a historic tax reduction bill in February 1964. Johnson asked Americans to spend the increase in their incomes that would result from the tax cut. Most economists concur that the Johnson-Kennedy tax cut was a moderately successful expansionary program.

Early in 1991, President George H. W. Bush signed into law a federal budget calling for tax increases, spending cuts, and other measures designed to reduce an expected increase in the debt over the next five years. Although government spending was not actually reduced very much, the previously planned increases were lowered. Economists identified the tax increases and spending cuts as a contractionary sign that eventually resulted in lower prices.

President John F. Kennedy, much like President Obama, attempted to strengthen the economy by using deficit spending.

Fiscal Discipline

President Bill Clinton's main economic goal was debt reduction. The first major accomplishment of the president's second term was an agreement with the Republican Congress on how to reach a balanced budget. Despite large tax cuts, the balance was achieved by trimming $263 billion from federal spending over a five-year period. During Clinton's administration, the country reached its first surplus in nearly thirty years. Some refer to the administration's policy as one of fiscal discipline.

Since the financial crisis of 2007 to 2010 and the recession that came with it, called the "Great Recession," the American people have been angry about fiscal irresponsibility. The nation had just experienced the consequences of the overlending and overborrowing of money for homes. People were angry at the banks who loaned the money because the complexity of the structure of the deals played a role in the economic turmoil that followed.

A new call for fiscal responsibility came in the form of a new political movement called the Tea Party, which organizes rallies calling for reduced government spending and lowering the national debt and lower taxes. While the Tea Party is not an official political party, its influence is great, having arguably swayed the 2010 election cycle.

A Challenge

Imagine it is the year 2040, and you are an influential member of Congress. The president has informed Congress that the country's economic output of $38 trillion is just not high enough. The president wants Congress to come up with a basic plan that would increase this figure significantly. Newer members of Congress are looking to you to provide leadership. They have never dealt with such complicated economic calculations.

You tell them not to worry. The answer is quite simple if you know some basic economics. What do you say to the other members of Congress? Answer: You remind the members that to increase economic activity the government must use an expansionary fiscal policy. By increasing government spending in areas such as the environment and national defense, the country certainly could increase economic activity. The government could also give businesses and individuals a tax break. But these businesses and individuals must spend the money in the economy. Otherwise the plan will backfire.

Using Technology to Keep an Eye on Spending

More than ever before, average citizens can act as watchdogs over fiscal policy. The Internet has allowed for a degree of transparency never before known. There are countless blogs and other Web sites that track government spending to make sure that your tax dollars are being put to good use. In fact, the administration of President Barack Obama even established its own Web site to allow citizens to see where money related to the Recovery Act is being spent.

Other government Web sites such as USASpending.gov allow you to track general spending dollars in numerous areas

Recovery.gov is the Web site that the Obama administration set up to allow people to track spending related to the Recovery Act.

such as construction contracts, higher education grants, and housing assistance. However, citizens shouldn't rely on the government to be self-policing. Non-government sponsored Web sites keep an eye on wasteful spending. Organizations like Citizens Against Government Waste keep an eye on what's called "pork barrel spending." This type of spending is done

44

by local politicians to bring money to their district in exchange for favors from residents. Most pork barrel spending only benefits those communities and not the nation as a whole. Other pork barrel spending projects seem so trivial that people question whether they benefit anyone at all. Instead, it is seen as wasteful and careless distribution of tax dollars.

There are even applications for your smart phone that can track government spending. Apps for devices such as smart phones and tablet computers allow you to track spending by department, region, and type. With interactive features and graphs, they're often more informative and helpful than general Web sites for accessible information about where your tax dollars are going.

CHAPTER **FIVE**

HOW YOU CAN HELP

Most people would agree that the government does a good job of providing goods and services. You may also think that the government has a pretty good handle on the budget. Or maybe you have some spending or taxing suggestions. Whatever your views, who couldn't use a little extra help? Just like people, the government can always benefit from new ideas. And who better to provide input than young citizens with a fresh outlook. If you would like to get involved in how the government spends, taxes, and manages its finances, here are some ideas to get you started.

Encourage Voting

Have you ever heard an adult complain about the way government money is being spent? Or perhaps the complaint is about taxes. Voting is one way citizens can participate indirectly in important spending and tax legislation decisions. Encourage voting for local representatives like your mayor or city or town councilors. Don't forget your governor, state legislators, and state senators.

The president is our highest elected federal official. The presidential election is held every four years. Every election is important, even if it is not a presidential election. Adults should vote at every opportunity. Important spending and

The greatest power citizens have over their government's fiscal responsibility is getting out and voting and encouraging others to vote.

taxing decisions are going on at every level of government. Let adults know they can have a say in the way the government taxes and spends by electing individuals who best represent their views.

Raise Your Voice

Maybe you think that the federal government should spend more money on the poor or that less money should be allocated to international affairs. Perhaps you are interested in the way your state is going to spend its surplus this year. A new youth center in your city might be your local lobbying point. Let your views be heard.

Thanks to modern technology, it is easy to contact your government officials. Social media is a great way to quickly voice your concerns. The great thing is that most elected officials have easily located social presences on sites like Facebook and Twitter. But don't forget that there is nothing like a good old-fashioned letter. Most officials will actually write you back.

Even though you can't vote yet, you can easily participate in government. Ask your parents if you can attend a local election debate or open forum. Don't be afraid to get involved. Does the candidate believe in a balanced budget, or is he or she a big spender? Find out. Ask candidates the following questions:

- What changes will you make in the city (or state) budget if you are elected?

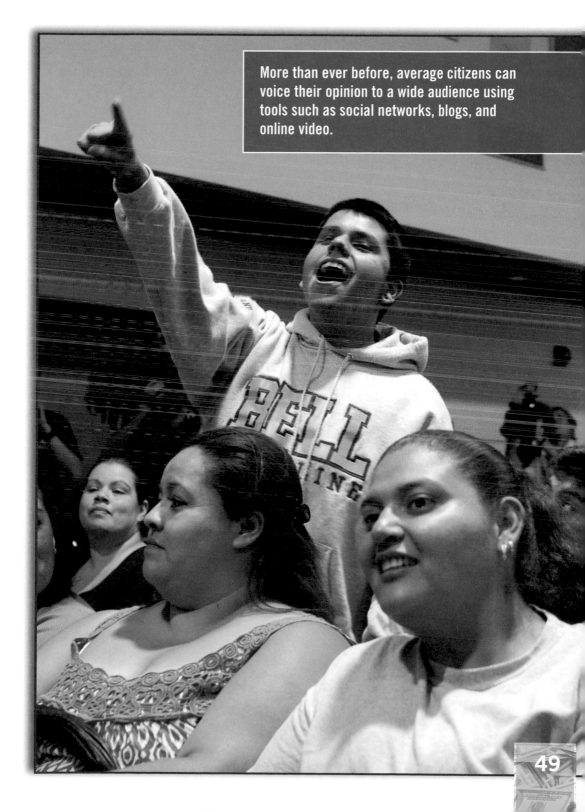

More than ever before, average citizens can voice their opinion to a wide audience using tools such as social networks, blogs, and online video.

- Do you think local taxes should be raised? If so, what would you do with the extra funds?
- Do you think citizens should receive a tax reduction?
- What is one item you would reduce spending on and why?
- What is one item you would increase spending on and why?

Attend your local county and city council meetings. Here the discussion and voting will be on specific topics. The topic could be almost anything: making plans for a new subdivision of homes, buying equipment for the firehouse, or building a new town tennis court. Find out what is going on in your local area.

What You Can Do

It has been in all the papers—your local town council has proposed to tear down the historic community center. It will be replaced with a new $5 million community center complex. There is so much concern over this proposal that the town council has scheduled an open forum for townspeople to share their views. What do you do?

Answer: You can do a lot. First of all, how do you feel about the proposal? Do you think it is a good use of funds? Then speak up. You might share with the council the things you and your friends would like to see in the center. Tell them that a pool, study room, and basketball court would be used a lot by people your age. Or maybe you think the new center is a bad idea.

TREASURY DEPARTM

Social media has enabled people, especially young people in America, to have a voice about how the government and the Treasury Department manage the government's money.

The historic community center is more than adequate for the town. The meeting rooms are used by young people and adults. The basketball court is old but spacious. Speak out. Mention all the fantastic things the town could do with $5 million: a shelter for the homeless, a community food bank, or a new park with outdoor play equipment. For $5 million, you may be able to provide all three.

Remember, the U.S. government is your government. And you are one of the leaders of tomorrow. Your actions will continue to ensure a strong, prosperous, and financially sound government.

Using Social Media for Change

You may not agree with the way your government handles taxes and government spending but feel powerless to do anything. After all, the government is a huge, faceless system that can only be swayed by the voices of millions of people. While this may be true, now, more than ever before, you have the means to influence masses through the power of the Internet and social media.

Social tools such as blogs and social networks are excellent ways to give yourself a platform to speak your mind about the way your politicians are governing. In fact, during the 2008 election, CNN hosted the CNN YouTube Debates in which citizens broadcast their questions directly to the candidates using the video sharing site YouTube. Also, the candidates each used their own Facebook pages to stay in touch with voters.

GOVERNMENT "BY THE PEOPLE, AND FOR THE PEOPLE"

A democratic government is ruled by the people, and not by a king, a dictator, an elite group, or the military. Leadership is given to people if the majority of the citizens vote for them to have it. In a democracy, every citizen is entitled to certain rights and freedoms. In our country, the federal government must provide and protect these rights and freedoms. It was written into our national constitution that every citizen of the United States of America is entitled to these rights and freedoms.

However, each citizen who is entitled to these rights and freedoms must also uphold them. For a democracy to work properly, every citizen must participate in it. Being an active citizen means more than just being alive, and you can choose to be an active citizen in many ways. Besides obeying the laws, you can be part of the process that creates new laws. Besides paying taxes, you can have a voice in how that money gets spent by the government. When you're a little older, you'll be able to do more than just vote. You'll be able to help the political party of your choice win elections. Getting involved in the government's business is how this country got started in the first place.

The basis for this democratic form of government was officially set down in the U.S. Constitution, a document that formed the foundation for the nation's laws. Over time the Constitution required changes and improvements. The rights of citizenship needed to be extended to all Americans. Originally, the Constitution did not outlaw slavery. Only white men who owned property could vote. The authors of the Constitution provided a system that allowed changes, called amendments, to be made to the document. The federal government amends the Constitution to provide laws for all citizens that are more just, creating a more fair and equal society.

The Thirteenth Amendment to the Constitution, added in 1865, outlawed slavery. The Nineteenth Amendment, added in 1920, gave women the right to vote. Speaking of voting, you probably know that you need to be at least 18 to vote. What you may not know is that eighteen-year-olds were not always allowed to vote. The Twenty-sixth Amendment created the voting age in 1971. These amendments are examples of a democracy that works to improve the lives of its citizens. Over time, the U.S. Constitution has proved that citizens of the United States are able to govern themselves using elected representatives to speak for them and make laws for the whole nation.

Social media works the other way, too. Instead of politicians using it to speak to the American people, you can use it to speak to them. If you feel strongly about a cause, say raising or lowering taxes, you can stay connected with like-minded people by joining their social networks. On the other hand, if you have some new ideas of your own, you can create your own network for others to join. The larger your following, the greater the chance your voice will be heard by the decision makers in Washington.

borrowing Related to finance, using the wealth of another person, entity, or government temporarily in exchange for interest.

budget deficit This type of deficit is defined as an excess of expenditures over revenues.

contractionary policy Policy tending to cause contraction, or to reduce the size of the money supply.

corporate income tax The taxes received from or the tax rate assigned to companies legally structured as corporations.

federal government In the United States, the central and highest ruling body.

federal taxes The taxes paid to a federal government by its citizens to fund goods and services such as roads and the military.

fiscal policy The rules by which a government enforces its budget.

goods and services In terms of economic output, goods and services refer to that which is produced by a nation's economy.

income tax The money paid to a government by an individual or business based on earnings.

inflation The phenomenon caused by too much money chasing too few goods that results in a general increase in prices of goods and services over time.

interest rates The rates at which money is borrowed.

Internal Revenue Service The part of the Treasury Department of the federal government that is responsible for collecting taxes.

national debt The amount of money that a nation owes to other nations or individuals.

New Deal The economic policy enacted by Franklin Delano Roosevelt from 1933 to 1940 that was designed to strengthen the economy during the Great Depression.

progressive taxation A tax system in which the rate increases as taxable income increases.

proportional taxation A tax system in which the rate is the same for all income levels.

recession A period of economic contraction or decline.

regressive taxation A tax system in which the rate decreases as taxable income increases.

sales tax A percentage of a good or service that is paid upon sale to a government.

Social Security A social welfare system in the United States designed to help and give economic security to the elderly.

spending The act of distributing money for goods or services with the hope of stimulating the economy.

Treasury bonds Long-term financial obligations issued by the Treasury Department that pay interest.

Department of the Treasury
1500 Pennsylvania Avenue NW
Washington, DC 20220
(202) 622-2000
Web site: http://www.treasury.gov
The Department of the Treasury is responsible for America's economic and financial systems, and is an influential participant in the world economy.

Federal Reserve
20th Street and Constitution Avenue NW
Washington, DC 20551
Web site: http://www.federalreserve.gov
The Federal Reserve, or the Fed, is the central bank of the United States.

National Governors Association
Hall of the States
444 N. Capitol Street, Suite 267
Washington, DC 20001-1512
(202) 624-5300
Web site: http://www.nga.org
The National Governors Association provides addresses and phone numbers of all state governors' offices.

Senate and House of Representatives
50 F Street NW, Suite 700
Washington, DC 20001
(202) 248-5261
Web site: http://www.congress.org
At this site, you can enter your zip code and gain access to your senator and congressperson. Along with the official e-mail and address information, their voting records are provided.

Statistics Canada
150 Tunney's Pasture Driveway
Ottawa, ON K1A 0T6
Canada
(800) 263-1136
Web site: http://www.statcan.gc.ca
An excellent source of statistics on Canadian government finance
    revenues and federal spending.

U.S. Conference of Mayors
1620 Eye Street NW
Washington, DC 20006
(202) 293-7330
Web site: http://www.mayors.org
The U.S. Conference of Mayors provides access to your mayor
    and local government. Highlight your city to find e-mail
    addresses, mailing addresses, and a description of your local
    government.

U.S. House of Representatives
Washington, DC 20515
(202) 224-3121
Web site: http://www.house.gov
One of the two houses of the United States Congress, which also
    includes the Senate.

White House
1600 Pennsylvania Avenue
Washington, DC 20500
Web site: http://www.whitehouse.gov
A great Web site providing information on the inner workings of the
    White House. The site provides a quarterly newsletter, *Inside the*

White House, just for kids. You can e-mail the president's and vice president's offices with your concerns.

Web Sites

Due to the changing nature of Internet links, Rosen Publishing has developed an online list of Web sites related to the subject of this book. This site is updated regularly. Please use this link to access the list:

http://www.rosenlinks.com/dol/tags

FOR FURTHER READING

Bedesky, Baron. *What Are Taxes?* New York, NY: Crabtree, 2009.

Chatzky, Jean Sherman, and Erwin Haya. *Not Your Parents' Money Book: Making, Saving, and Spending Your Own Money*. New York, NY: Simon & Schuster for Young Readers, 2010.

Cooper, George. *The Origin of Financial Crises: Central Banks, Credit Bubbles and the Efficient Market Fallacy*. New York, NY: Vintage, 2008.

Davies, H., and David Green. *Banking on the Future: The Fall and Rise of Central Banking*. Princeton, NJ: Princeton University Press, 2010.

Donovan, Sandra. *Budgeting*. Minneapolis, MN: Lerner Publications, 2006.

Hall, Margaret. *Money*. Chicago, IL: Heinemann Library, 2008.

Hammonds, Heather. *Budgeting*. South Yarra, Victoria, Australia: Macmillan Library, 2006.

Kennedy, Roger G. *Wildfire and Americans: How to Save Lives, Property, and Your Tax Dollars*. New York, NY: Hill and Wang, 2006.

Kiyosaki, Robert T. *Rich Dad, Poor Dad for Teens: the Secrets About Money—That You Don't Learn in School*. Paradise Valley, AZ: Running, 2009.

Kowalski, Kathiann M. *Taxes*. Tarrytown, NY: Marshall Cavendish Benchmark, 2006.

McLean, Bethany, and Joseph Nocera. *All the Devils Are Here: The Hidden History of the Financial Crisis*. New York, NY: Portfolio/Penguin, 2010.

Mullins, Eustace Clarence. *The Secrets of the Federal Reserve: The London Connection*. Carson City, NV: Bridger House, 2009.

Musell, R. Mark. *Understanding Government Budgets: A Practical Guide*. New York, NY: Routledge, 2009.

Paul, Ron. *End the Fed*. New York, NY: Grand Central, 2009.

Piper, Mike. *Taxes Made Simple: Income Taxes Explained in 100 Pages or Less*. Chicago, IL: Simple Subjects, LLC, 2008.

Reichblum, Charles. *What Happens to a Torn Dollar Bill?: Dr. Knowledge Presents Facts, Figures, and Other Fascinating Information About Money*. New York, NY: Black Dog & Leventhal Press, 2006.

Ritholtz, Barry, and Aaron Task. *Bailout Nation: How Greed and Easy Money Corrupted Wall Street and Shook the World Economy*. Hoboken, NJ: John Wiley & Sons, 2009.

Rothbard, Murray N. *The Case Against the Fed*. Auburn, AL: Ludwig Von Mises Institute, 2007.

Roubini, Nouriel, and Stephen Mihm. *Crisis Economics: A Crash Course in the Future of Finance*. New York, NY: Penguin, 2010.

Thakor, Manisha, and Sharon Kedar. *On My Own Two Feet: A Modern Girl's Guide to Personal Finance*. Avon, MA: Adams Media, 2007.

Wattenberg, Martin P. *Is Voting for Young People?* New York, NY: Longman, 2006.

Young, Mitchell. *Government Spending*. Detroit, MI: Greenhaven, 2009.

INDEX

About the Authors

Clive Nichols is a writer living in New Jersey.

Marie Bussing-Barks is a writer living in New York City.

Photo Credits

Cover, pp. 6, 18, 27, 34, 46 © wwww.istockphoto.com/ FreezeFrameStudio; pp. 7, 11, 12, 14–15 © AP Images; p. 9 Steven Puetzer/Photonica/Getty Images; p. 19 MPI/Archive Photos/Getty Images; pp. 22–23 Andy Nelson/Christian Science Monitor/Getty Images; pp. 28, 50–51 Bloomberg via Getty Images; p. 31 Shutterstock.com; p. 35 Chip Somodevilla/ Getty Images; p. 36 Tim Gidal/Hulton Archive/Getty Images; pp. 38–39 © David Young-Wolf/PhotoEdit; p. 41 Arnold Sachs/ Archive Photos/Getty Images; p. 47 Baltimore Sun/MCT via Getty Images; p. 49 Armando Arorizo/Landov; interior graphics © www.istockphoto.com/mecaleha.

Editor: Nicholas Croce; Designer: Nicole Russo; Photo Researcher: Peter Tomlinson